SAY YES TO STRESS

THE ANXIOUS WAY TO SUCCESS

**MARCEL FEIGEL ·
BRIAN BUSSELLE**

Drawings BILL KERWIN

Featuring THE HIGH ANXIETY DIET

FREDERICK MULLER
London Melbourne Auckland Johannesburg

First published in Great Britain in 1988 by
Frederick Muller, an imprint of Century Hutchinson Ltd,
Brookmount House, 62-65 Chandos Place,
London WC2N 4NW

Century Hutchinson Australia Pty Ltd
PO Box 496, 16-22 Church Street, Hawthorn,
Victoria 3122, Australia

Century Hutchinson New Zealand Limited
PO Box 40-086, Glenfield, Auckland 10, New Zealand

Century Hutchinson South Africa Pty Ltd
PO Box 337, Bergvlei, 2021 South Africa

British Library Cataloguing in Publication Data

Feigel, Marcel
    Say yes to stress: how to lose weight by worrying.
    1. English humorous cartoons – collections from individual
    artists
    I. Title   II. Busselle, Brian   III. Kerwin, Bill
    741.5′942

    ISBN 0-09-173579-3

Printed in Great Britain by
Richard Clay Ltd, Chichester, Sussex

CONTENTS

HOW TO TURN A NAIL-BITING LIFESTYLE INTO A SLIMMER, MORE SUCCESSFUL YOU

FEATURING THE HIGH ANXIETY DIET
THE FIRST DIET THAT LETS YOU EAT AS MUCH AS YOU LIKE

Never mind what you've been told.

Far from being bad for you, anxiety is really your *secret* friend.

A friend who can help you unlock the secrets of success.

This book will show you how.

Starting with simple, everyday anxiety, you will progress to stress in the office, in the bedroom and even during yoga classes.

Once you've mastered the basic stress techniques, you will then graduate to the complex world of advanced anxiety.

And as an added bonus you'll learn how stress can keep you beautifully slim through THE HIGH ANXIETY DIET, the first diet that lets you eat as much as you like as long as you worry about it.

In short, here is everything you need to know to turn panic into a successful lifestyle.

WHY STRESS IS GOOD FOR YOU

We're always told how people "suffer" from stress, as if it were some terrible disease.

Or we read about stress related illness when doctors can't find any other reason for whatever's wrong.

But we're never told about the good that stress does.

After all, life without stress would be placid.

Or worse, complacent (the very word feels like flopping down in an easy chair ready for a full evening of viewing).

Or worst of all, smug.

Stress on the other hand is dynamic.

Stress keeps you on your toes, drives you into action, makes you an achiever and can keep you slim (smugness won't keep you slim, that's for sure).

The trouble is people have been taught to be afraid of stress so they try to avoid it. They run away from it. All this does is create angst and angst is where all the trouble comes from.

NOW WHAT IS IT I'M SUPPOSED TO BE WORRYING ABOUT TODAY ?..

6

The answer lies not just in accepting stress but in embracing it whole-heartedly and letting its magic work for you.

By developing a vigorous 'hands on' approach to stress, by becoming a stress *seeker*, you develop dynamic tension that in turn releases a flood of positive energy.

By learning to love stress you will have all that radiant energy at your command.

What's more, anxiety – your secret friend – will be watching and guiding you through the swings and arrows of life.

For the anxious, the world is full of riches. And it's getting wealthier every day.

Never has there been so much to worry about. And the beauty of it is that all that worry can work to your benefit.

All you have to do is say "Yes" to stress.

7

COMPLACENT   V   ANXIOUS

COMPLACENT	ANXIOUS
Wakes up as soon as the alarm rings and jumps out of bed.	Wakes up before the alarm, but doesn't get out of bed until long after it's rung.
Eats slowly, often at the same place.	Eats quickly, sometimes standing up. Often gulps because he's in a hurry, or out of habit.
Books holidays 6 months in advance.	Books the day before and then worries about whether he's going to the right terminal.
Relaxed about the future.	Terrified.
Always finishes what he starts.	Starts numerous projects then gives up halfway through.
Gave up cigarettes a year ago.	Gives them up every month.
Always answers yes when asked at rock concerts if he feels "all right".	Doesn't go to rock concerts because they're always sold out by the time he gets around to them.
Rarely has an overdraft and then only up to £150.	Has two overdrafts (both of which he's trying to extend) an Access card, American Express and Barclaycard and a cash-flow account which is never in credit.
Always leaves his keys and wallet in the exact same place so he can find them immediately.	Usually a desperate, last minute scramble to find them. Or leaves the house quite contentedly only to return five minutes later in a panic.
Stays with the same partner all his life but fantasizes about other women.	Changes partners regularly and fantasizes about his first grade teacher.

GETTING INTO THE STRESS HABIT

MAKING LISTS

One of the best ways of developing a general level of anxiety is by making lists.

Be sure to make one every day. And leave nothing out. Nothing is too trivial to include, birthday cards to distant cousins, phoning the pub to see if they still have your umbrella – throw it all in. The longer the list the better.

And always be sure to add a few too many items (for you must never actually go through the list).

It's also good to include one or two long range items. So after:

> Take shirts to cleaners
> Pick up pint of milk
> Buy condoms

You can add:

> Learn French

You've probably wanted to learn French for some time and haven't done anything about it. And you probably won't do anything about it today, but seeing it on the list day after day is a good way to activate a little guilt.

WHERE ON EARTH
DID I PUT MY LIST?

SHOPPING

THE MISPLACED WALLET

When you go to bed at night, place your wallet in a pocket where you normally wouldn't put it.

Next morning, when you hit your first financial port of call, you'll instinctively reach for the pocket where you normally keep it. Seeing it's not there, your blood pressure will quickly double its normal rate; your heart beat will shoot up to an aerobic level roughly equal to running eight miles in two minutes, and you may even hyper-ventilate.

At the same time your hands will be going through their own motions roughly approximating a tic tac man who has suddenly lost his marbles.

This is an excellent way of getting a quick burst of High Anxiety. But it's not recommended for newcomers as it can sometimes be fatal.

An interesting variation can be performed with your keys.

THE TAXI

Arrange to have lunch with an old friend, preferably someone you haven't seen for some time. And give yourself just enough time to make it if you hurry and everything goes exactly right which includes getting a taxi the *second* you leave the building.

The chances are that you'll get stuck in heavy midtown traffic. This is beneficial in two ways. On the one hand you're anxious about the time that's slipping away which is particularly useful for breaking up cholesterol around the arteries.

But that anxiety is compounded by the relentless ticking of the meter to remind you that you're losing money in the bargain. This helps release carbohydrates because your anxiety is working in overdrive.

Once you finally get to your destination, you'll probably have a great deal to talk about which will cut fairly deeply into your lunch hour and necessitate another taxi (this is known as 'the double taxi'). And that's when the pounds really come rolling off.

Calorie Loss
The taxi   400 calories
The double taxi   900 calori

LEAVING THINGS UNTIL THE LAST MINUTE

Your stress level, like your sugar level, can easily go down, especially at night.

That's why it's important to recharge it in the morning. One of the best ways to get it soaring is by getting a late start and then having to rush.

In stress terms this is the equivalent of the healthy breakfast. Because it sets you up for the rest of the day.

Once procrastination becomes part of your routine you'll wonder how you ever managed without it. And you'll find that it slots in neatly into different parts of your life — from arriving late at airports to starting your christmas shopping at the last minute.

LISTENING TO OTHER PEOPLE'S PROBLEMS

People are always ready to tell you their troubles, especially when you don't have time to listen. They have an uncanny ability to catch you just as you're going somewhere.

Because they get very easily offended, your only choice is either to listen attentively or patiently explain that though you haven't got the time this second you'd be happy to get together some other time when you could really discuss the situation in depth.

Either way you get a workout.

Listening to the problems of others especially when you do it out of politeness, while appearing concerned, fuels a slow burning anxiety that's all the more effective because it can't be seen.

THE ANXIOUS PHONE CALL

VISITING THE BANK MANAGER

STRESS AND (FITNESS)

Let's be honest, anxiety alone can only do so much.
If you really want to stay trim then you must
exercise.

And here we come to the best of both worlds – anxious
exercise.

For if exercise tones the body, sharpens the mind and
helps you burn up calories, then just think of the
fantastic results you can achieve by *worrying while
you exercise.*

JOGGING

AEROBICS

YOGA

Yoga is an ideal exercise for anxious people because it gives you the most time to worry.

It's particularly useful for slimming and is recommended as part of the High Anxiety Diet.

Never mind what yoga instructors say about clearing the mind and letting tension float away – that's just a fad which probably started in LA.

It's true there are some Swamis who advocate stressless yoga, but have you seen them? Most are definitely on the chubby side.

There is no reason why yoga and worry can't go together. After all, they have for over two thousand years. Its what the Indians call Lean Yoga, now sometimes referred to as Yuppie Yoga. But whatever you call it, it can go a long way to make you the Skinny Minny you always wanted to be.

SHE'S BEEN HAVING QUITE A FEW HEADACHES LATELY...

I KNOW I SHOULDN'T HAVE HAD THAT THIRD BRANDY AFTER LUNCH

DID HE SAY BREATHE IN OR OUT?

HE HASN'T CALLED FOR THREE DAYS NOW

OH NO I THINK I PUT MY SILK BLOUSE ON A HOT CYCLE IN THE WASHING MACHINE

THAT REMINDS ME WE REALLY MUST GET THAT CEILING RE-DECORATED

OH GOD WHY DOES THAT FAT WOMAN KEEP EYEING ME?

I DIDN'T LIKE THE WAY SHE WAS LOOKING AT BOB.

HE NEVER BUYS A ROUND

SHE HATES-SHE LOVES ME - SHE...

WAS THAT MY LEOTARD OR MY SPINE?

NOW, DID SHE ASK FOR LEMONS OR MELONS?

IS YOGA REALLY THE ANSWER TO MY PROBLEMS?

PERHAPS SHOULD I HAVE TAKEN UP WOODWORK

GOD! I FORGOT MUM'S BIRTHDAY AGAIN

DEEP RELAXATION

All yoga exercises end with deep relaxation. This is a good time to get to grips with your deepest worries.

One of the best things about anxiety is that it doesn't have to be recent. You can reach back as far as you like and draw on buried neurosis to help you release buried fat.

Remember how your classmates used to pick on you because you were no good at games. Or the way you never gave yourself any respect because nobody else did. And how no one used to go out with you more than twice and you thought it was just because of your spots. Well, bring it all out, visualising everything as vividly as if it were yesterday and feel that lithe, head-turning figure that's always been there trying to get out, becoming a reality.

Calorie Loss
150 Calories

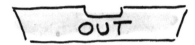

STRESS AT THE OFFICE

Offices can be very anxious places.

Either you're on your way up which is bound to be stressful because you can be sure there will be people trying to block your way.

Or you're on the way down which is even more stressful.

Or you're in the middle, not sure of which way you're going, if you're going anywhere. This can also be fraught.

On the other hand, you could be in a very quiet office where there isn't much happening.

In which case you're really in trouble. Because that's the most stressful of all.

ARRIVING LATE FOR A MEETING

ASKING FOR A RAISE

SPECULATING WITH COMPANY FUNDS

Calorie Loss
2000 calories

CAUGHT OUT AT LORDS

STARTING AN AFFAIR WITH THE CLIENT'S WIFE

ENDING AN AFFAIR WITH THE CLIENT'S WIFE

WRITING OFF THE COMPANY CAR

RUNNING YOUR OWN COMPANY FROM THE OFFICE

LOVE IS...

A CONSTANT WORRY!

GIVING BUT NOT EXPECTING

GIVING PLEASURE

39

TOTAL TRUST

EVER HOPEFUL

BEING THE PERFECT GENTLEMAN

FULL OF SURPRISES

IS BLIND

KNOWING YOUR HEART BELONGS TO JUST ONE PERSON

Calling out the wrong name in bed, either in your sleep or during the height of sexual abandon, can be extremely useful. Because it's a dramatic way of stimulating post-coital anxiety which can offset the giddy relaxation that too often follows sex.

It can also stimulate some fairly heated pillow talk; that is, if the pillows are still there.

But best of all, it will lead to an anxious relationship which is an indispensable part of any true stress seeker's life.

Perhaps you're fortunate in having an anxious relationship already. Or you may even have several. If so, then you're in luck. If you don't, then what are you waiting for? There are plenty to go around.

So why should you feel deprived when it can do such wonderful things for your figure.

Calorie Loss
In your sleep   250 calories
In the throes of passion   600 calories

45

ADMITTING YOUR SHORTCOMINGS

IN THE WEE SMALL HOURS

(NIGHT-TIME ANXIETY)

Nocturnal anxiety follows a path of its own.

Finally freed from the grind of the daily run-around, you can now lie in bed, wide awake, counting your worries instead of sheep.

First get the minor worries out of the way. This allows you to come to grips with deeper, more brooding anxieties.

The ones that, like vampires, only come out at night.

I'VE BEEN IN BED FOR HALF AN HOUR AND I'M STILL AWAKE!

THE KIDS AREN'T HOME YET I WONDER IF ANYTHING'S HAPPENED?

THESE BANK STATEMENTS AREN'T LOOKING TOO HEALTHY.

WHAT HAVE I REALLY ACHIEVED WITH MY LIFE?

THIS IS RIDICULOUS. I MIGHT AS WELL GET UP AND HAVE A DRINK.

I WONDER IF I TURNED OFF THE XEROX MACHINE AT THE OFFICE.

I CAN'T BELIEVE IT'S 6.15 AND I'M STILL AWAKE.

ADVANCED STRESS

As you adjust to your new lifestyle, you may find that you need a regular, concentrated dose of high anxiety to maintain the momentum, just like some people grow to need a high fibre diet.

If that's the case, then you might have to make some changes in your life like...

INVITING THE IN-LAWS FOR THE WEEKEND

GOING FREELANCE

One of the best ways of ensuring an uninterrupted worry flow is by going freelance.

Because the beauty of freelance is that not only do you not know when you're going to get your next job, but you don't know when you're going to get paid for the last one either.

If you're not in a position to go freelance then you may just have to settle with changing jobs.

MOVING HOUSE

AND GETTING A DIVORCE

In stress terms, both moving house and getting a divorce are classics, and can take their place besides other classics like forgetting to post a winning pools coupon, losing the book of matches with the phone number of the new love of your life, or finding out that your sole client has been bought out by Toshiba.

The beauty of moving house and getting a divorce is that they create a total upheaval in your life and, if you're fortunate, one can lead to another.

But if you had to choose, divorce would win

simply because its effects last longest. As that sage of stress, Woody Allen, remarked, a wife is only a wife for the duration of marriage. An ex-wife is with you forever.

ASKING THE WORKMEN IF THEY WOULD MIND 'AWFULLY' TURNING THE RADIO DOWN

OPENING A WINE BAR IN IRAN

BUYING A MEDICAL DICTIONARY

Needless to say, anxious people are very anxious about their health.

Sceptics dismiss this as hypochondria. But anxious people know better. They know they're coming down with something. And what's more, it's serious.

Anxious people know that there are no such things as minor ailments or common colds. These are just thin disguises for potentially chronic, degenerative diseases.

After all, today's mole is tomorrow's malignant Melanoma.

That's why it's important to get the disease before it gets you. That calls for painstaking medical detective work.

By keeping a medical dictionary by your bedside table you'll be able to spring into action at a second's notice with a full list of terrible but obscure diseases that are notorious for evading medical diagnosis.

In time you will also realise the importance of keeping up with medical journals. Because new illnesses are coming out all the time.

And how can you tell when you've got something if you don't even know what it's called.

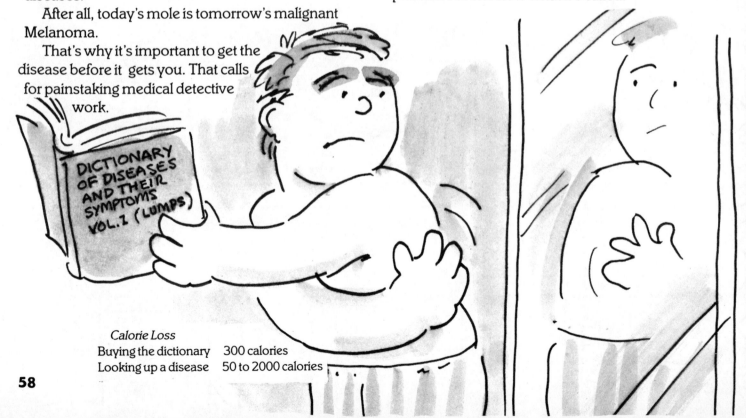

Calorie Loss
Buying the dictionary   300 calories
Looking up a disease   50 to 2000 calories

THROWING A DINNER PARTY FOR PEOPLE WHO DON'T LIKE EACH OTHER

EATING FOOD AFTER THE SELL-BY DATE

NOT PAYING YOUR TAX FOR EIGHT YEARS

MOVING TO NEW YORK

LIFE'S LITTLE GIFTS TO STRESS LOVERS

It's not just the big things that cause anxiety.

Little things are also important, particularly little irritations. These musn't be underestimated, for though minor in impact, these *frissons of friction* play an important part in fueling stress.

Fortunately, modern urban living abounds in irritants, from buses that are 30 minutes late to public telephones that don't work. These all help you sustain a constant stress level.

Another big plus with little irritants is that some of them you can actually buy. Most of these are 'convenience' products supposedly designed to make life easier. This is why it makes it even more stressful when they don't work the way they're supposed to.

Some people think the reason you can never find the beginning of a roll of sticky tape or the straw on a juice container is that they've been badly designed. The truth is that manufacturers have come round to recognising the importance of stress and now build it into their products.

OPENING A BOTTLE OF WINE ON YOUR FIRST DATE.

OPENING A CARTON OF MILK

TRY PULLING IT OUT AND THE WHOLE ROLL COMES TUMBLING OUT.

FINDING THE END OF A ROLL OF STICKY TAPE.

GOOD MORNINGS BEGIN

BREAKFAST

EASY TO OPEN JAM JARS.

AW - NUTS !

ENVELOPES THAT DON'T STAY STUCK.

WHY DO SHOELACES ALWAYS SNAP WHEN YOU'RE IN A HURRY ?

WHERE DID THE STRAW GO ?

THE MAP

1

2

3

4

5

6

8

9

RECOMMENDED PROFESSIONS

ACCOUNTANT TO THE 'FAMILY'

BOMB DISPOSAL

WAR CORRESPONDENT

DRIVING INSTRUCTOR

STOCKBROKER

PAKISTANI UMPIRE

MODERN STRESS

Like cockroaches and flu germs, stress is infinitely adaptable.

It relishes new situations and thrives on new technology, the more state of the art the better.

Anything new presents a golden opportunity for stress to assert itself. Which is why new strains are being developed every day.

Here are a few that are going around at the moment.

BEING LET DOWN BY YOUR MATE

Calorie Loss
500 calories

LOSING YOUR FILOFAX

HE MEMORIES

YOU'RE OUT!

TRYING TO REMEMBER WHETHER YOU RECORDED OPEN UNIVERSITY OVER THE CUP FINAL

Calorie Loss
700 calories

HAVING A TEENAGER WHO IS ALWAYS PHONING CHATLINES

LOSING YOUR CONTACT LENSES WHILE HANG GLIDING

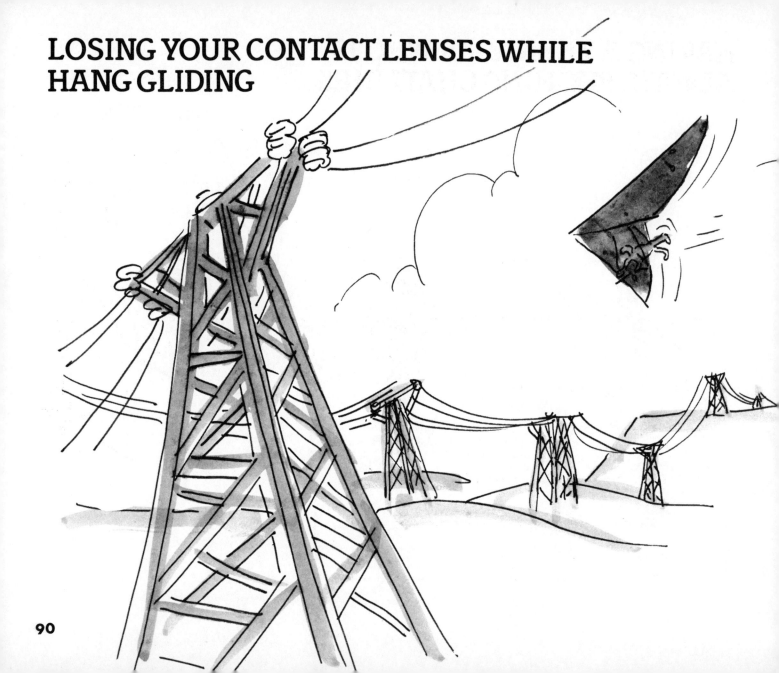

WHAT TO READ
WHAT TO WATCH

Required Reading

1. Bank Statements

2. School Reports

3. Gas or electric meters

4. Amnesty International Report

5. CBI Business Forecast

6. All documents leaked

   to the *Guardian* or

   the *Observer*

7. Labels on convenience food

8. Publications by Friends of the Earth or Greenpeace

9. The predictions of Nostradamus

10. Instruction Manuals

11. The Complete Works of Kafka

12. Novels given by well meaning relatives who say

    "you must read this"

13. Repeat gift subscriptions to the *Readers Digest*

14. John Le Carre novels after page 20

What To Watch

1. News Programmes.
2. *Panorama, World In Action, Horizon.*
3. Anything to do with the nuclear industry.
4. Films about people who have disappeared and never been seen again.
5. Being forced to watch *Blind Date* by your teenage daughter.
6. Programmes on unemployment, Ulster, world famine, the deterioration of inner cities, the growth of terrorism, the contamination of the earth and the Synod's view on gay vicars.
7. All reports on cutbacks in the NHS.
8. The Eurovision contest.
9. Programmes about the decline of Britain, especially those that focus on all our brilliant inventions that we've given away.
10. Films like *Psycho, Airport, Towering Inferno* and *Midnight Express*. Argentinian films of social realism and Polish cartoons.
11. Reports about fraudulent tradesmen.
12. ITN job survey.
13. Anything to do with Aids.
14. Third repeat of *Man About The House*.

It's particularly useful to start the week with a strong dose of TV stress. And here the networks are only too happy to help. As Nancy Banks Smith, the *Guardian* television critic has pointed out, "It has long been traditional television practise to depress the hell out of the viewer on a Monday." Which is why they like to put on *Panorama, World In Action* and *Horizon* on the same day.

She goes on to say that *Horizon* in particular "offers unique scope for anxiety".
So take a tip from a pro. And remember, Monday evenings are strictly for staying at home.

FAMOUS PEOPLE WHO HAVE BENEFITTED FROM STRESS

Imelda Marcos
Having to make do in a new country with a deposed dictator and only three van loads of shoes has kept her young and vigorous.

Mel Brooks
Mr. High Anxiety himself. So impressed was he with this regime that he even made a film about it.

Maggie Thatcher
To look at her you would never think she was addicted to the boxes of Milk Tray her junior ministers are always leaving her but nevertheless she stays lean and alert. And it's all because the lady loves stress.

Woody Allen
Did you know that at one time he was fat and not very funny. Until he discovered the joys of stress.

Colonel Gaddafy
Going home at night, never knowing if your tent is going to be where you left it, breeds a sense of insecurity which has made him the international sex symbol that he is today.

Nancy Reagan
Acting as the president's cue card is enough to keep anyone cadaverously thin.

Elton John
Worrying about losing your hair while at the same time being anxious about losing your voice has kept him svelte and in top form.

John McEnroe
He used to be known as Mr. Nice Guy in his early days when he was ranked No. 285. Then he discovered stress and his career took off. Though now that he's become a daddy, parental complacency may have set in.

Lester Piggot
After a triumphant career in one of the world's most taxing professions, he has found anxiety to be just the ticket for keeping in good nick.

Elizabeth Taylor
How do you think she lost all that weight?

DOUBLE TROUBLE

Just as some vitamins are more effective when combined with others, the same can also be true of stress.

And there is a special breed who prefer their stress in multiple doses — the stronger the better.

These people, who make up a kind of elite, include high powered executives, politicians, Jewish mothers and racing drivers.

But be warned, Double Trouble is definitely not for everybody. The rewards may be great but most people can't stand the strain.

However, once you decide to start doubling up on stress, you'll be pleasantly surprised how easy it is to find.

After a while, you won't even have to look for it. It'll find you.

FALLING IN LOVE WITH A PAVEMENT ARTIST WHILE TRYING TO END A RELATIONSHIP WITH A DENTIST

Falling madly in love with someone who is *totally* wrong for you and who you're never sure you'll ever see again is very exciting. It can also be very stressful.

It could be some advertising smoothie you met at a wine bar. Or an actor working as a waiter. Or a pavement artist.

What's exciting – and stressful – is that everything is so uncertain.

Sometimes you may not see him for weeks and just as you're about to finally give him up, he suddenly appears with all the rakish, heartbreaking charm of an Irish poet.

This kind of relationship, if that's what you want to call it, is particularly good for losing weight. And sleep.

But you can become even slimmer if, while worrying about the pavement artist, you're also in the throes of breaking up with a dentist after three (or was it four?) uneventful years.

And you'll lose even more weight if you and he are entangled in a few cumbersome details like co-owning a time share in Tunisia. And if he still brings his laundry to your flat.

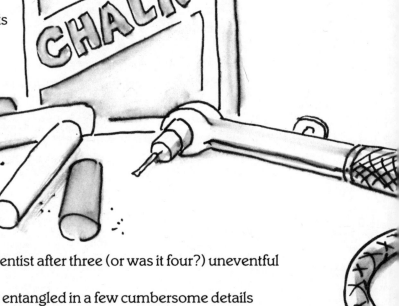

100

Calorie Loss
750 calories

LISTENING TO YOUR HORSE FALL AT THE LAST FENCE IN THE GRAND NATIONAL AND DRIVING INTO A LAMPOST

GETTING ON THE WRONG TRAIN THEN DISCOVERING THAT IN YOUR HASTE TO GET OFF YOU LEFT YOUR ATTACHE CASE BEHIND

HAVING A JEWISH SON WHO FAILS HIS DOCTOR'S EXAM AND THEN MARRIES A SHIKSA

DISCOVERING TWO MONTHS AFTER YOUR MOTHER'S FUNERAL THAT YOUR FATHER HAS MARRIED A 24 YEAR OLD BIMBO TO WHOM HE PLANS TO LEAVE HIS ENTIRE FORTUNE

THE HIGH ANXIETY DIET

THE MOST REVOLUTIONARY WEIGHT REDUCING IDEA OF OUR TIME

The High Anxiety Diet is the very first diet that lets you eat as much as you like.

No, your eyes didn't deceive you, we said as much as you like – of anything you like.

From cherry trifle to banana splits, deep dish supreme pizzas to croissants with butter and jam, you can have it all.

That's what makes The High Anxiety Diet not just a radical idea, but the most revolutionary weight reducing concept of our time.

Of course there is one *little* proviso.

You've got to worry. Most of your worrying will be done before eating, though it probably wouldn't hurt if you worried a little afterwards as well.

Naturally, the more you eat the more you'll have to worry.

And it shouldn't come as a total surprise to hear that you'll have to worry more after a double portion of deep fried prawns with chips than you would after a cottage cheese salad with Ryvita.

That's only logical. And the laws of anxiety are nothing if not logical.

So with the battle of the bulge, as with so many of life's conflicts, anxiety can be your ally.

HOW IT WORKS

The Most Revolutionary Weight Reducing Idea of Our Time

The High Anxiety Diet is the very first diet that lets you eat as much as you like.

No, your eyes didn't deceive you, we said as much as you like – of anything you like.

From cherry trifle to banana splits, deep dish supreme pizzas to croissants with butter and jam, you can have it all.

That's what makes The High Anxiety Diet not just a radical idea, but the most revolutionary weight reducing concept of our time.

Of course there is one *little* proviso.

You've got to worry. Most of your worrying will be done before eating, though it probably wouldn't hurt if you worried a little afterwards as well.

Naturally, the more you eat the more you'll have to worry.

And it shouldn't come as a total surprise to hear that you'll have to worry more after a double portion of deep fried prawns with chips than you would after a cottage cheese salad with Ryvita.

That's only logical. And the laws of anxiety are nothing if not logical.

So with the battle of the bulge, as with so many of life's conflicts, anxiety can be your ally.

CALORIE CHART

CALORIE RATING	FORM OF ANXIETY	REWARD	CALORIE RATING	FORM OF ANXIETY	REWARD
1 —100	Thinking about your next visit to the dentist	2 Smarties	1000 —1250	Extending your overdraft and starting an affair with your client's wife	German sausage with potato salad and cabbage
100 —200	Leaving your new umbrella on the tube	Half a chocolate bar	1250 —1500	Not declaring tax	Two stick shish kebab and rice with five glasses of Ouzo and Turkish delight
200 —300	Watching Panorama without a TV licence	Glazed donut	1500 —1800	Not declaring tax and getting a letter from IRS	Two fried eggs, bacon, sausage, beans, fried bread and black pudding
300 —450	Leaving for work without checking that everything is turned off	Cream cake	1800 —2000	Moving to New York with no contacts	Assorted stuffed bagels with potato latkes
450 —600	Spending £80 on a date and not getting anywhere	Spotted dick with custard	2000 —2100	Speculating with company funds	Madras curry with rice plus 3 stuffed parathas and two pints of Dortmunder
600 —1000	Forgetting your wedding anniversary and discovering you've been left out of your father's will	Paté and toast washed down with 2 bottles of wine			

110

CALORIE RATING	FORM OF ANXIETY	REWARD	CALORIE RATING	FORM OF ANXIETY	REWARD
2100 – 2200	Going freelance and eating prawns after sell-by date	Deep pan pizza and large coke	2350 – 2500	Forgetting to post winning pools coupon followed by anxious sex	Joint of beef with roast potatoes, yorkshire pudding and complete freedom of choice from the trolley
2200 – 2250	Being discovered in bed with somebody else by your partner	Bowl of borscht, chicken Kiev and bottle of Bulls Blood	2500 – 3000	Starting your Christmas shopping at 4.30 on Dec 24 and suspecting that the mole on your neck might be malignant	Saddle of rabbit, stuffed with a veal farci, pistachio and pine nuts served with a juniper berry sauce flavoured with gin and Irish coffee
2250 – 2300	Moving house	Stuffed Hogshead in apple sauce followed by fudge brownies	3000-5000	Losing your filofax, your spouse and your biggest client all on the same day	7 course blowout featuring "The Works" including champagne, unlimited wine, lager, port and stilton and After Eights
2300 – 2350	Taking the family for a sailing holiday after writing off the company car	Halfpound cheeseburger with large fries, ketchup, thick chocolate milkshake and blueberry pie			

111

PANIC

EXTREME - ANGST
ANGST
HIGHLY ANXIOUS
ANXIOUS
FRAUGHT
STRESSFUL
NERVOUS
TENSE
JITTERY
ON EDGE

Doctors still can't agree which is more stressful, angst or panic. While this highly charged debate rages on, all we can advise is that you sit tight and wait for the sequel to this book.